Lerner SPORTS

ALL-STAR
SMACK
DOWN

TINA CHARLES VS. LISA LESLIE

WHO WOULD WIN?

JON M. FISHMAN

D1736794

Lerner Publications ◆ Minneapolis

SPORTS THRILLS
MEET
RESEARCH SKILLS

Lerner SPORTS

Free Database Trial: **lernersports.com**

Lerner Publications Company
An imprint of Lerner Publishing Group, Inc.
241 First Avenue North
Minneapolis, MN 55401 USA

For reading levels and more information, look up this title at www.lernerbooks.com.

Main body text set in Aptifer Sans LT Pro.
Typeface provided by Linotype AG.

Library of Congress Cataloging-in-Publication Data

Names: Fishman, Jon M. author.
Title: Tina Charles vs. Lisa Leslie: who would win? / Jon M. Fishman.
Other titles: Tina Charles versus Lisa Leslie
Description: Minneapolis, MN: Lerner Publications, [2024] | Series: Lerner sports. All-star smackdown | Includes bibliographical references and index. | Audience: Ages 7–11 | Audience: Grades 4–6 | Summary: "Tina Charles and Lisa Leslie have dominated women's basketball from the center of the court. Compare their WNBA and Olympic careers, and decide which legendary center is the best"— Provided by publisher.
Identifiers: LCCN 2022046213 (print) | LCCN 2022046214 (ebook) | ISBN 9781728492346 (library binding) | ISBN 9798765602478 (paperback) | ISBN 9781728495866 (ebook)
Subjects: LCSH: Charles, Tina, 1988– —Juvenile literature. | Leslie, Lisa, 1972– —Juvenile literature. | Women basketball players—United States—Biography.
Classification: LCC GV884.C535 F57 2024 (print) | LCC GV884.C535 (ebook) | DDC 796.323092/2 [B]—dc23/eng/20221026

LC record available at https://lccn.loc.gov/2022046213
LC ebook record available at https://lccn.loc.gov/2022046214

Manufactured in the United States of America
1-53230-51207-2/28/2023

TABLE OF CONTENTS

Lisa Leslie

INTRODUCTION

HISTORY MAKERS

Los Angeles Sparks center Lisa Leslie made history on July 30, 2002. Her team faced the Miami Sol in Los Angeles, California. Leslie quickly gave the hometown fans something to cheer about.

» Fast Facts «

- ○ Lisa Leslie won two Women's National Basketball Association (WNBA) titles.
- ○ Leslie is a member of the Naismith Memorial Basketball Hall of Fame and the Women's Basketball Hall of Fame.
- ○ Tina Charles is the fourth WNBA player to score at least 7,000 career points.
- ○ Charles has won three gold medals in the Olympic Games with Team USA.

With less than five minutes to play in the first quarter, the Sol missed a shot. The ball bounced to Sparks player Latasha Byears. She threw a long pass to Leslie, who stood alone near center court.

Leslie dribbled to the basket. She leaped for a slam dunk. Fans jumped to their feet and cheered. Leslie had just made the first slam dunk in WNBA history!

The Sol won the game 82–73. But WNBA fans and players remember Leslie's dunk as one of the most exciting moments in league history. She was one of the WNBA's first true superstars.

Tina Charles

Lisa Leslie makes the first slam dunk in the WNBA.

Twenty years later, another center made a huge impact on the league. Seattle Storm center Tina Charles is a scoring machine. On July 24, 2022, the Storm faced the Atlanta Dream. Charles started the game with 6,986 career points.

Charles scored nine points in the first quarter. In the second quarter, she made a three-point basket. Then Storm teammate Epiphanny Prince had the ball. She passed it to Charles. Charles took a step and made another three-pointer.

As she ran down the court after scoring, Charles held up four fingers. With 7,001 career points, she had become the fourth WNBA player to score at least 7,000. Charles had reached an incredible milestone. But does her career point total make her better than Leslie? Read on to find out. Let the smackdown begin!

Tina Charles (right) has not won a WNBA title, but she is one of the league's greatest scorers.

CHAPTER 1

Leslie played center for Morningside High School in Los Angeles, California.

BECOMING SUPERSTARS

Lisa Leslie was born in Gardena, California, on July 7, 1972. Gardena is near Los Angeles, California.

Lisa was taller than most kids her age. In sixth grade, she stood 6 feet 5 (1.9 m). She didn't play basketball, but many people asked her if she did. Being tall is a big advantage in basketball. Tall players can reach high to grab rebounds and shoot over shorter players.

Lisa began playing basketball in seventh grade. She shot

and dribbled with her left hand. Most of her teammates played right-handed, so Lisa taught herself to do the same. Her ability to play with both hands helped her succeed throughout her career.

At Morningside High School, Lisa became the best player on her team. She led Morningside to the 1989 California state championship. The next season, Lisa tried to set a new scoring record. She scored 101 points in the first half of a game against a team from Torrance, California. The US high school girls record for points in a game was 105. But Lisa couldn't break the record because the team from Torrance refused to play the second half.

Lisa in her Morningside Monarchs uniform

After high school, Leslie played at the University of Southern California. She was the team's best player for four seasons. She set all-time conference records for points, rebounds, and blocks.

The WNBA's first season was in 1997. Leslie was one of the first 16 players to join the new league. With the Los Angeles Sparks, she was ready to take on the world's best players.

Leslie gets ready to grab a rebound during a USC game. She was usually the tallest player on the court.

Leslie helped the Sparks reach the playoffs 10 times in her 12 seasons with the team.

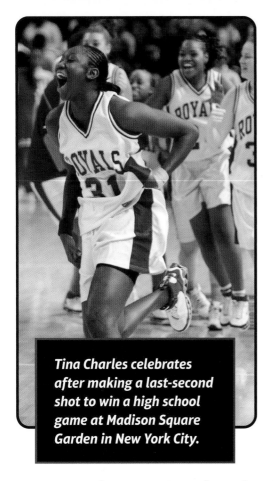

Tina Charles celebrates after making a last-second shot to win a high school game at Madison Square Garden in New York City.

Tina Charles began playing basketball much earlier than Leslie did. Tina was born in Jamaica, New York, on December 5, 1988. She practiced her basketball moves on a toy hoop at home. She started playing with a team in first grade.

Tina played other sports, including softball and soccer. But basketball was her best sport. She was tall and played with skill. When she was 12, she received a letter from Stony Brook University. The school's basketball team hoped she would play for them after high school. In the years to come, she received similar letters from many other schools.

Tina attended Christ the King High School in Queens, New York. She led the team to two state championships. In 2005–2006, Tina's senior season, Christ the King didn't lose any games. The team won 57 times in a row.

She had similar success in college. Charles attended the University of Connecticut. She helped the Connecticut

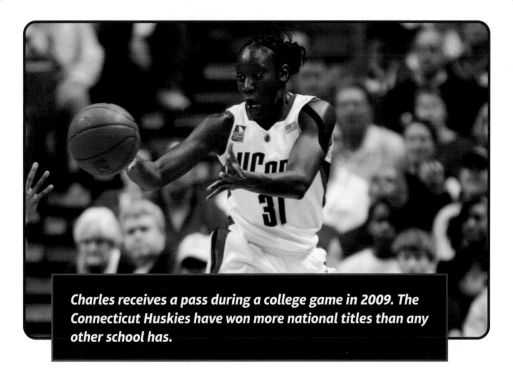

Charles receives a pass during a college game in 2009. The Connecticut Huskies have won more national titles than any other school has.

Huskies win national titles in 2009 and 2010. She won many awards in college, including the 2010 Naismith Women's College Player of the Year award.

Charles was ready for the next level. She entered the 2010 WNBA Draft. The Connecticut Sun chose her with the first overall pick.

CONSIDER THIS

Leslie and Charles both played four seasons of college basketball. Leslie racked up 2,414 points and 321 blocks. Charles had 2,346 points and 304 blocks.

CHAPTER 2

Leslie (center left) and Team USA sing the US national anthem after winning the gold medal at the 1996 Olympic Games.

GREATEST MOMENTS

Leslie was a worldwide basketball star before she ever played in the WNBA. In 1996, she led Team USA to the gold medal match at the Olympic Games in Atlanta, Georgia. Leslie and her teammates faced Brazil.

Brazil had won the women's basketball world championship in 1994. But at the Olympics, they were no match for Team USA. A Brazil player took a shot near the basket. Leslie leaped and smacked the ball out of bounds. Moments later, she received a pass about 10 feet (3 m) from the basket. She spun to her right for an easy score.

Team USA won the game 111–87. Leslie set a game record with 29 points. But her Olympic career was just getting started. She helped Team USA capture the gold again in 2000, 2004, and 2008.

Leslie fights for the ball during the gold medal game against Australia at the 1996 Olympic Games.

Leslie had almost as much success in the WNBA. The
Houston Comets won the first four WNBA championships.
But then Leslie and the Sparks took over. They won WNBA
titles in 2001 and 2002. They returned to the Finals in 2003.

*Leslie holds the 2001 WNBA championship
trophy after defeating the Charlotte Sting
in the WNBA Finals.*

Tina Charles (left) shoots over a leaping France defender at the 2012 Olympics.

Leslie led all players in points and rebounds, but the Sparks fell to the Detroit Shock.

For Tina Charles, 2012 was a huge year. In August, she and Team USA played France for the Olympic gold medal. Near the beginning of the game, France missed a long shot. Team USA's Maya Moore grabbed the rebound.

Charles raced to the other end of the court. Moore saw her and threw a long pass over three French players. Charles grabbed the ball and quickly bounced it off the backboard for a score. France couldn't keep up with Charles and her teammates. Team USA won the game 86–50.

That same month, Charles also reached a WNBA milestone. She played her 100th WNBA game on August 19. Her 12 rebounds helped the Sun beat the Indiana Fever 73–67. Charles became the fastest player to grab at least 1,100 career rebounds in WNBA history. After the season, she won the WNBA MVP award.

Charles (top row, seventh from left) and her 2012 Team USA teammates and coaches

Charles (left) receives the 2012 WNBA MVP award.

CHAPTER 3

Leslie dribbles past a defender to take a shot in the 2005 WNBA All-Star Game.

WINNING BY THE NUMBERS

Leslie and Charles have taken different paths in the WNBA. Leslie played in the league for 12 seasons. She spent all of them with the Sparks.

Leslie's career was full of awards and amazing stats. She played in eight WNBA All-Star Games. She won the All-Star Game MVP award three times.

Leslie was the WNBA's first great scorer. She finished the season in the league's top 10 in scoring nine times. Leslie was the first WNBA player to reach 3,000 career points. She also became the first to reach 4,000 and 6,000 points.

In 2010, Charles won the WNBA Rookie of the Year award. The award marked the beginning of a great career. After the 2013 season, the Sun traded Charles to the New York Liberty for two players and a draft pick. She spent six seasons in New York. In 2020, the team traded her to the Washington Mystics for a player and four draft picks. Charles has also played for the Phoenix Mercury and Seattle Storm.

Leslie holds up three fingers as she accepts the WNBA All-Star Game MVP trophy for the third time.

Charles joined the Seattle Storm in 2022. The team plays at Climate Pledge Arena in Seattle, Washington.

CONSIDER THIS

Leslie averaged 17.3 points, 9.1 rebounds, and 2.3 blocks per game in her career. Charles has averaged 18.2 points, 9.3 rebounds, and one block per game.

Charles has led the league in scoring three times. After the 2022 season, she had 7,115 career points. Tamika Catchings is ahead of her with 7,380 points. Charles could pass Catchings soon to capture third place on the all-time scoring list. How high on the list can Charles go? WNBA fans can't wait to find out.

After more than ten years in the WNBA, Charles has no plans to retire.

CHAPTER 4

Lisa Leslie reaches up to block a shot during a 2004 game against the Phoenix Mercury.

AND THE WINNER IS

Does this all-star basketball smackdown have a clear winner? Decide for yourself! Sports fans often have different opinions, and that's fine. Forming your own ideas is part of the fun of sports.

Before you choose, think about the facts again. After the 2022 season, Leslie and Charles had both played 12 WNBA seasons. Charles holds the edge in scoring average and total points. But Leslie was better at blocking shots. And don't forget that Leslie won two WNBA titles. Charles is still hoping for her first title.

Charles grabs another rebound. She has led the WNBA in rebounds four times.

Leslie retired from playing in 2009, but she has stayed busy. She wrote a book about her life, commented on basketball games on TV, and became one of the owners of the Sparks. In 2015, she joined the Naismith Memorial Basketball Hall of Fame and the Women's Basketball Hall of Fame.

Charles is still playing, so her amazing stats could become even better. She is already one of the league's all-time best scorers. If she can add a WNBA championship to her three Olympic gold medals, she will become a legend.

With the edge in WNBA titles, Leslie is the winner of this smackdown. Do you agree? Think it over and make your choice!

Leslie speaks at the Naismith Memorial Basketball Hall of Fame in 2015.

Leslie's height, skills, and hard work made her one of the WNBA's all-time greatest players.

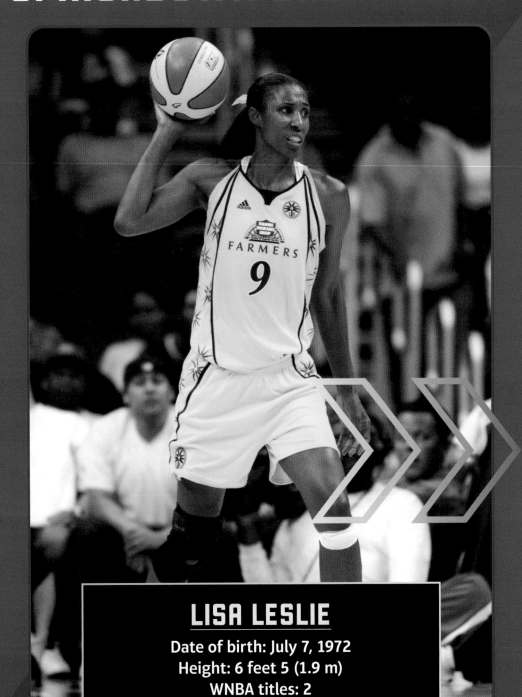

LISA LESLIE

Date of birth: July 7, 1972
Height: 6 feet 5 (1.9 m)
WNBA titles: 2
WNBA MVP awards: 3
Olympic gold medals: 4

TINA CHARLES

Date of birth: December 5, 1988
Height: 6 feet 4 (1.9 m)
WNBA titles: 0
WNBA MVP awards: 1
Olympic gold medals: 3

GLOSSARY

block: when the ball is knocked away by a defender before reaching the hoop

center: a player who usually stays close to the basket and the middle of the court

conference: a group of sports teams that play one another

draft: when teams take turns choosing new players

dribble: the act of moving a basketball forward by bouncing it

milestone: an important achievement or moment while moving toward a goal

MVP: short for most valuable player

rebound: grabbing and controlling the ball after a missed shot

rookie: a first-year player

slam dunk: a shot made by jumping high into the air and throwing the ball down through the basket

three-point basket: a shot taken from behind the three-point line on a basketball court that counts for three points

title: a championship win

LEARN MORE

Davidson, Keith B. *WNBA*. New York: Crabtree, 2022.

Lowe, Alexander. *G.O.A.T. Basketball Centers*. Minneapolis: Lerner Publications, 2023.

Naismith Memorial Basketball Hall of Fame
https://www.hoophall.com/

Scheff, Matt. *NBA and WNBA Finals: Basketball's Biggest Playoffs*. Minneapolis: Lerner Publications, 2021.

WNBA
https://www.wnba.com/

Women's Basketball Hall of Fame
https://www.wbhof.com/

INDEX

PHOTO ACKNOWLEDGMENTS

Image credits: Lisa Blumenfeld/Getty Images, p. 4; Steph Chambers/Getty Images, pp. 5, 7; Lisa Blumenfeld/NBAE/Getty Images, p. 6; AP Photo/Julie Markes, p. 8; AP Photo/Tony Duffy/Allsport, p. 9; Ken Levine/Getty Images, p. 10; Todd Warshaw/Allsport/Getty Images, p. 11; Corey Sipkin/NY Daily News Archive/Getty Images, p. 12; Jamie Schwaberow/NCAA Photos/Getty Images, p. 13; Rick Stewart/Allsport/Getty Images, p. 14; Al Bello/Allsport/Getty Images, p. 15; Harry How/Allsport/Getty Images, p. 16; Christian Petersen/Getty Images, pp. 17, 18; AP Photo/Jessica Hill, p. 19; AP Photo/Bob Child, p. 20; AP Photo/Susan Walsh, p. 21; Christopher Mast/Getty Images, pp. 22, 29; AP Photo/Gregory Payan, p. 23; AP Photo/Chris Carlson, p. 24; Tim Clayton/Corbis/Getty Images, p. 25; AP Photo/Charles Krupa, p. 26; AP Photo/Jerry S. Mendoza, p. 27; Brandon Parry/Southcreek Global/ZUMAPRESS.com/Alamy Stock Photo, p. 28.

Cover: Francis Specker/Alamy Stock Photo, (Lisa Leslie); AP Photo/Lindsey Wasson, (Tina Charles).